FAREWELL
TO TARGET AT
HICKSVILLE

FAREWELL TO TARGET AT HICKSVILLE

Johnny Wong

iUniverse LLC
Bloomington

FAREWELL TO TARGET AT HICKSVILLE

iUniverse books may be ordered through booksellers or by contacting:

iUniverse LLC
1663 Liberty Drive
Bloomington, IN 47403
www.iuniverse.com
1-800-Authors (1-800-288-4677)

Because of the dynamic nature of the Internet, any web addresses or links contained in this book may have changed since publication and may no longer be valid. The views expressed in this work are solely those of the author and do not necessarily reflect the views of the publisher, and the publisher hereby disclaims any responsibility for them.

Any people depicted in stock imagery provided by Thinkstock are models, and such images are being used for illustrative purposes only. Certain stock imagery © Thinkstock.

ISBN: 978-1-4917-1302-0 (sc)
ISBN: 978-1-4917-1303-7 (e)

Printed in the United States of America.

iUniverse rev. date: 06/04/2014

• • • •

I just finished applying for a position at Target. I picked up the red phone and told the operator, "I just completed the application process."

"We are conducting interviews next week," she said. "When would be a good time for you to come in?"

"How about Wednesday at 11:00 a.m.? Would that be okay?"

"That will perfectly be fine. We will give you a call."

"Thank you very much and have a nice day."

I never wished to celebrate too early. Ever since leaving college in 1985, I had close to about three hundred interviews, resulting in very little success. Some sounded impressing and promising, but actually getting the position was similar to hitting a split-finger fastball. The split-finger fastball is considered the most difficult pitch to hit. It seems like the perfect ball to swing at. Unfortunately, at the last second, the ball drops from the strike zone, and most batters strike out foolishly.

At the same time, I was feeling optimistic. When I applied for the Target at Elmhurst at Queens Boulevard about four times in the past, they once guaranteed to interview me but never delivered. I had just gotten back from Kansas City. Things didn't work out over there, and friends disappointed me. Once again, I was back in New York for the fourth time.

The day of the interview, similar to a general planning out his strategy, I opened up a new, recently purchased white shirt. I put on my favorite red tie and khaki dress pants. It was mid-June. As I stepped out the house, I felt the blazing sun glaring on my shoulders. I smelled green grass. It all meant summer was in the air.

Target happened to be located at North Broadway Mall, once called Mid-Island Plaza, in Hicksville, New York. The last time I had been to that shopping mall, it was September 1983. I was going out with a girl named Carol.

I got to the bus stop at Flushing Main Street. About twenty-five people were waiting in front of me for the N20 bus to the Hicksville train station. Of all the buses, this one was considered the most crowded. We were packed like sardines in a tin can.

I sat next to the window on my way to Hicksville and got to observe the scenery of Nassau County. Nassau and Orange Counties probably had the highest per capita income of any residential places in the United States.

As the vehicle slowly approached C.W. Post Long Island University, memories of Carol kindled in my heart. I would say she was your average Italian, all-American girl—New York Yankees and Islanders, Billy Joel, Beatles, hamburgers, meatballs, hot dogs, blueberry pie, and America's favorite pastime.[1] When I first encountered her, she was studying to be an actress. She invited me to one of her plays. She portrayed her role to absolute perfection.

"Broadway Mall," the bus driver said.

---

[1]   Leon Uris, Exodus (New York: Bantam Books, 1958), 4.

Once I got off, like stepping toward a museum park, I could hardly believe that twenty-four years ago seemed like a different universe. These days, it was labeled as Mid-Island Plaza because the town of Hicksville happened to be midway between Nassau and Suffolk Counties. To my surprise, the shopping mall had decreased a little in size. The architecture seemed pretty amazing with its many retail businesses and restaurants.

I walked into the human resources office.

Alice, the receptionist, was very pleasant and nice to me. "Have a sit."

About a half hour later, the human resources manager, Ronald, called me into his office. He was very friendly, nice, and down-to-earth.

One question seemed to rattle across his mind. "Johnny, how flexible are you? Can you work on weekends, Saturdays, Sundays, nights, days, or holidays?"

"Oh, I am very flexible. I could work any time of the day."

"Since you don't reside in Long Island, would it be a major problem for you getting here?"

"Definitely not. There's the N20 Hicksville Nassau County transportation that takes me directly to the mall. I could also travel on the Long Island Railroad."

"I also take the Long Island Railroad. Johnny, due to your flexibility, I am going to offer you a position right now."

Wow, I couldn't believe what I was hearing. My head almost felt like striking the ceiling.

He didn't bother to check my employment references. Not only was he nice, but when a manager gives you a position on the very first day, that tells you what kind of character he possesses.

After his statement, I somehow sensed his employees must have a lot of good things to say in regard to him. He shook my hand and told me to go next door to obtain a drug test. He said they'd call me for orientation. Before I left the human resources office, I somehow knew we had struck a wonderful friendship that would last until the final days at Target.

Unlike most employees, I sensed right away that he wasn't there to collect that fat check, as most people are. I understood deep down inside that he cared. He took the time and reached out to his coworkers whenever they encountered issues.

The following Wednesday was orientation. Ronald's assistant gave a speech, a general outline in regard to store policies and how to interact with customers. We saw a video on sexual harassment. It demonstrated interaction between men and women, on what to do or not do, such as inappropriate contacts or speeches. That was far from my concern. The main issues happened to be racism against black people. Struggling with these issues for about twenty-one years, we had made little progress and then fell away time after time.

Some of the words kept echoing inside. "No matter what you do, if caught in a verbal or physical confrontation, you have everything to lose. They've got nothing to lose. If you are not ready and don't feel comfortable sitting, standing, or staring at a black person, then quietly get up and remove yourself from that situation."

The last time I was employed was back in 2004, so it had been a while. Target was going to be the testing ground. How individuals and blacks viewed me made an impact on what type of person Johnny Wong was. Was he a cruel, evil, revengeful type that would have arguments or fights with coworkers?

Since I had suffered the mental illness OCD for so many years, I was hoping everybody, or at least most people, would be understanding. It wasn't something that went away overnight. It would take many years, step by step, one day at a time.

I needed to remind myself that blacks are not perfect. Not all would treat me nicely. They are similar to most people on the earth. They are not Superman. I didn't have high expectations for them. They're just ordinary person who have problems like us. I had lost many jobs in the past because of confrontations with African Americans. Somehow deep in my mind, I wasn't going to let history repeat itself.

The following day, I reported to work. The first big test was in the back stockroom. The first person to introduce himself to me, Abdul, was a black fellow. To my surprise, I struck up a pretty interesting conversation with him. Later on, he introduced Omar, an Arab. Both were willing to teach me. Not only were they helpful, they went out of their way to assist me in whatever they knew how. Words have a way of expressing itself through them. Even if I created about a hundred errors in pushing or pulling the items or stocking products on the wrong shelf, they still continued to treat me nicely, never having any angry words at me.

At this particular moment, I noticed right away that the job was boring as hell. They told me to work on the back stock order, that is, removing items from the cart and placing them on the correct shelf.

Out of the blue, as I was climbing the ladder to place a product on the shelf, a cool dude named Peter Son came up to the ladder and extended his hand to greet me.

"Wow, what a start. What a way to go. Today is a brand-new day." For those who are familiar with baseball, I was batting close to three hundred.

I told him, "I'm nervous, being the first day on the job, and I don't know too much about the stockroom. I am slow. I made huge mistakes, similar to being the new kid on the block."

"No, that's quite okay. You have nothing to be afraid of. I am here with you. If you work beside me, you'll do fine."

He was kind of like the Lone Ranger assisting me in a crisis. He taught me how to point the gun and equipment we handled at Target. He told me to aim at the code bar, advising me on how to position myself at certain directions and angle and standing at a certain range of your body. Peter let me know that firing the gun (pressing the button) would receive a funny sound. If no sound appeared, something went wrong. The materials wouldn't process.

Next step he demonstrated was how to pull, taking items off the stockroom. Because I was a rookie, I wasn't used to the challenge, but on the other hand, he did possess a lot of confidence in me. He explained certain numbers when punched into the gun, plus counting how many items were left in the boxes.

There was another fellow, a pretty cool dude, Lamont, but I wasn't very close with him. On the one hand, he always looked out for me, asking if I took the forty-five-minute lunch and fifteen-minute breaks.

The next day, I was introduced to the big chief, Bob, in the back stockroom. When I first laid eyes on him, I knew right away that he was a great guy. He was your average person. He was very down-to-earth and never had any harsh words with anybody in Target. First day working alongside him, I felt like Superman.

"You're doing one hell of job with the back stock, Johnny," he said.

From what I viewed of this person, difficult as it may seem, I doubted if he had any enemies in Target. It was like he was telling me, "Johnny, welcome to the back stockroom. Don't worry. We'll take good care of you. Today, you're one of the family."

Fritz was the next cool dude. I was a little afraid. Beginning new in the stockroom, I feared asking him any questions. He looked tough from the ghetto and shocked me a little.

But he told me, "If you have any questions, don't be scared of letting me know."

One major thing we shared in common was that both of us were big Mets fan.

I said, "I was born before your time when the Mets had the best pitching staff. It consisted of Tom Seaver, Jon Matlack, and Jerry Koosman."

The conversation got really hot as we said they were the best team in winning the World Series back in 1986 against the Boston Red Sox, four games to three. This was how we described game six at Shea Stadium. The Red Sox were ahead by one run. Mookie Wilson headed up to bat with the tying run on third base. Boston was one out away from capturing the World Series. The count was full, three balls and two strikes. Mookie fouled the last couple of pitches out of the place.

Then a mighty strange thing occurred. He hit a slow grounder toward Boston's first baseman, Bill Buckner. Right away, it looked like a routine play.

"Mookie has good speed," the announcer said.

At the last minute, he took his eyes from the ball and looked at Mookie. Instead of playing it safe by placing the glove on the ground, the ball took a funny hop and ran through his legs. The tying run scored. The Mets, again alive, went on to win game six and were champions.

The next dude who came into the picture was none other than Big Sean, and nobody messed around with him. He was a big, tough dude, and he studied martial arts, so nobody dared to get on his case. Interestingly, he said he had some Chinese blood. He was probably from Jamaica. There are quite a few Chinese Jamaicans beside Jews, Indians, and whites. I assumed the Chinese were usually the wealthiest because almost everyone loves Chinese food.

I spoke with a black fellow while working in Boston in 1989. I said to him, "Us Chinese don't give anybody a hard time."

He immediately responded, "But you people give us good food."

Lamont told me to go for lunch around two. We went to the food court at the mall, which was very crowded as hell. Everything was considered high price. They didn't don't need to worry about the Chinese restaurant stealing business from other fast-food places. It didn't matter what kind of individual. They all enjoyed Chinese food.

I had fried rice with vegetables, along with some delicious steaks and shrimps.

He asked me, "What's your name?"

"Johnny."

Next thing, he noticed my Target badge. He pointed a sign to me: "All employees at mall get 10 percent discount."

I mentioned to myself, "Boy, there's a real treat."

As I headed back toward work, I met another funny character, Little Sean, to differentiate himself from Big Sean. Little Sean was wild dude. His mouth was similar to a firecracker. For him, life was assumed to be a joyous, big roller coaster ride. Most occasions, I hardly sensed he was ever in a bad, depressing, or angry mood. I never saw him firing full ammunitions, that is, giving harsh words to people. The idiot considered himself as working in a three-ring circus.

Next he asked me, "Have you ever been in bed with any women?"

"No."

"You're way behind the game, batting below three hundred."

Because I never had sex with any woman, the count was oh and two, stating I had two strikes in life. He let me knew that he wanted to set me up. Hell, I didn't care if he offered some soul mama, Indian, Latino, or fair-skinned women. To be honest with all you folks at Target, I once worshiped white women like diamonds and gold. I spent money, cooked for them, and purchased gifts for this group of girls. Never once did they say I was cute or good looking. For over thirty years, these women had the nerve to take. They grabbed from me and never gave me anything back in life. So what the hell when these blacks, Indians, and Latinos said, "You're cute and handsome." That showed these nonwhite girls were very pleasant to hang out with, while white girls happened to be very racist toward us Asian men.

Later on, I found it hard to concentrate on my work. An ugly battlefield waged in my mind. To those who don't know anything regarding mental illness, I struggled with obsessive-compulsive disorder (OCD), a very severe sickness. There were days that, if anyone hurt my feelings or directed angry words against me, I found it extremely difficult in getting through the day without obsessing over the issues.

Two months ago, after I got back from the International House of Prayer in Kansas City, many of the young kids there assisted them financially. They never bothered to get back in touch with me. In my brain, I was waging an angry confrontation with this group of people. The only solution to get rid of the obsessive images was to get some payback time with them, either by sending them angry mail or email or saying an evil prayer for them.

Then my mind switched back to reality. Peter Son told me, "By a certain time, for example, ten, noon, four, and six, those are the times we need to pull the items from the shelf and put them in the cart. People working out on the sales floor will roll it out."

Inside the stockroom, I imagined a twenty-first century battlefield. Fritz, Big Sean, Little Sean, Peter Son, Frank, and Lamont, we were similar to modern-day warriors. Our only weapon was our handheld electronic device. The batteries inside were considered to be our source of ammunition.

I could hear the Big Chief Bob from the other side of the room, giving the order. "Okay, the customer is waiting for the order. Please don't screw up. Big Sean, you work on the trailer. Little Sean, you take the pet items. Frank, take care of the bed and toy. Fritz, work on the pillow, bed, and chemical. Peter Son, please stay close with Johnny since he's the new kid on the block. Give him a chance because he doesn't know what the hell he's doing."

One Saturday, either in August or July, one or two guys called in sick. Only Bob and I were running the show, dropping the café from our gun and pulling the items from the shelf. For the next three to four hours, we were like robots, both sweating like an angry dog.

In any retail business, no matter what, the customer always comes first. They were usually right. It was considered bad blood to start an argument. Never curse at the clients. The result could be termination. If they needed something, it wasn't good policy to keep them waiting for a long period of time.

The sales manager and stock people working on that day were getting excited and very anxious. They kept complaining to Bob, "What's taking so long in getting the orders out? The customer needs it right away!"

Bob and I were doing our best. Out of his compassion and kindness, he didn't say a word to me. Instead, he was really pissed off with the manager above him.

He just said, "Just tell them they have no other choice but to be patient. We're doing our best to get the merchandise out. It's only Johnny and me. He's doing a hell of job."

Finally by four o'clock, Little Sean came in with his imaginary fire truck. He brought out the hoses to put out the burning flame. Boy, was I glad to see him. He saved our teeth.

Some night, when I filled for Bob and Sean, it was between the both of them. They had to drop a couple of café and pulled a huge number of stuff to the sale floor. Those times, I stayed with Little Sean and Peter Son to give them some help. Some situation. I could tell Sean seemed a little upset when I explained to him that I needed to catch the Nassau County bus, which only came at every half hour. As days went by, he began to slowly understand, traveling from Hicksville to Flushing, a rather very long trip if one didn't own a car.

As a good gesture on some nights, I offered to assist Peter Son. There was usually a big smile on his face. I highly respected him.

I never gave me the heavy load or things too high to reach if it happened to be beyond my reach.

His motto was, "Johnny, you must come first before anything else."

After our job was over, when we headed toward the human resources office, I often joked about the Mets and Yankees with him. I usually told him, "The Mets possessed a better team because their players represented the city of New York, while the Yankees don't give a damn. Instead to me, they're very selfish. They collect big bonuses, carrying a fat wallet stuffed with millions of dollars inside." I always said to him, "The Mets will beat the Yankees in the World Series if they ever meet."

His response was, "Oh yeah, Johnny, we'll see."

I always admired all those guys in the back stockroom. Frank was a martial arts expect. He knew everything concerning Bruce Lee, Jackie Chan, and Jet Lee. He told me, "Bruce Lee was the best. He's the legend. No one could compare to him." He liked Jackie Chan, saying, "He's a funny character."

Before I moved to another position in the store, I said to those guys, "This was back in 1977 before all you were born. I went to Thomas Edison High School, about 95percent blacks, and I was the only Chinese dude."

They said, "Johnny, Johnny, you know that dude Bruce Lee? Did he beat up the black dude Jim Kelly? Yo, Johnny. Bruce Lee is not dead. He's still alive. He's hiding somewhere. When he comes back to life, he's going to be the black Bruce Lee."

Afterward, they all started to laugh like crazy. They could stop laughing for over five minutes. They thought it was a really cool joke. Somehow I considered all of those guys as Chinese soul brothers. In some way, they all looked after me. Even good old Bob stuck out his life for me.

One summer day, when all of NYC was flooded, most of the people couldn't rely on public transportation to get to work. I started calling to Target at six, six thirty, and sixty forty-five. It was about four times. No one answered. Finally, I tried at ten thirty, Alice the receptionist said I didn't call, so she put me down for "no show, no call" on my employment record. When I tried to explain everything to her, she was kind of angry and kept telling me, "Everybody who couldn't make it called … except you."

From that point on, I knew I was dealing with a very angry person who was not very pleasant, so I spoke with Bob on the phone. He said to me, "You have absolutely nothing to worry about Johnny. Just ignore what Alice said. When you come in tomorrow, I'll have everything taken care of, okay?"

The next day on the job, he told me, "I've taken care of everything. You won't be on record."

"Well, that's just a real treat from a very cool fellow. I wish every boss in Target would be like Bob," I said to myself.

Little Sean might be pretty sneaky and wise, but that dude normally looked out for me. He warned me about climbing ladders and told me to be extremely careful picking up heavy boxes. Once I cut myself with a blank accidentally. I tried ignoring the pain, telling him, "It's only a small cut. It's only bleeding a little."

He responded, "No, you don't want to let germs get into the finger. You could get infected. Please go to human resources and ask for a Band-Aid."

The other day, they posted everybody's score on the wall. I happened to be the last guy on the list. As soon as Bob came in, he said to me, "Don't be afraid. Not a thing to worry over. I'll work with you."

I told Peter Son, "Hey, I'm afraid I might be out of a job because I scored 88. I needed to score 95 percent accuracy in pulling the products."

"From now on, just watch and work with me," he said.

Once or twice, when we had to pull the products from the shelf, I had to move a lot of the boxes out of the way in order to scan the bar code. As soon as he came over, he was shaking his head, embarrassing me in front of the other guys.

"Come on, Johnny. You're wasting a lot of time. You could have moved to a less crowded location."

I answered angrily to him, "Why can't you just come down? I can't help it. There's too many boxes, and they're very heavy for one person to move."

Another time, I wasn't concentrating on the job. I was thinking about girls in the one-piece swimsuit in the shopping mall pool. I scanned the bar code outside the carton, took some stuff out, and forgot the number of counts.

"You got to concentrate on what you're doing," he said.

"Hey, I am doing the best I could."

"If that's the best you could do, then that's fine."

Later on, we took a glance at each other and started to smile. He laughed and shook his head. I could read his mind. I guessed it said, "This guy Johnny has to stop thinking about girls in general and concentrate on his work."

The next morning at work, we were in for a shock. Omar introduced me to a new black fellow, Brian. Because I had an illness, I didn't know what to do or expect. I just froze there for a couple of seconds. He was quiet. He didn't want to shake my hand. It was to be my first real test, a black not being friendly or nice to me.

Omar told me to work with him. I had him doing the back stock. When the boxes were falling down from the tub, he just stood there and watched me picking it up. He didn't even bother to ask me if he could help to grab the fallen carton with his hand.

"Boy, this guy isn't very nice," I said to myself. "He didn't even say a word to me."

Finally, I asked him, "Can you please give me a hand with the boxes?"

Before I showed him how to point the gun at the label to scan the order number, he said to me he knew how to use it already. When Little Sean and some of the other fellows came in, he started to socialize with them. I couldn't read his mind. Did he have racism toward Asians, or was he being shy and quiet?

This wasn't going too well. I was losing the battle. For the next couple of days, I tried my best to avoid him. Whenever he was working on the top floor, I went downstairs. If he were next to me, I went somewhere else. I'm pretty sure you heard that familiar expression, "The harder you try to avoid a particular individual, most likely, he will cross your path." This means that, more than 90 percent of the time, you're going to run into that person.

The first time I met him, he struck me out by throwing a nasty screwball, a ferocious curveball, and a split-finger fastball. Here I was in a lousy situation, a black person giving me the cold shoulder. The old saying that blacks are everywhere on Planet Earth is totally true. Even going to the Asian countries in Hong Kong during 1992, I didn't see many in the tourist section. Even in China nowadays, there are blacks studying to learn to speak, read, and write Chinese. Some resided in Hong Kong and China, holding high government jobs.

The next time I confronted him, I tried to sweet talk and be nice to him. "You might be racist against Chinese people, but I'm still going to be your friend. And if you had questions, you could come to me for assistance."

It turned out to be the worst move. He countermoved by using his queen to corner trap my king, putting me in a dangerous position. He held the upper hand, a good position. It was check on me. I had no other choice but to move my king out of position. I thought of using harsh verbal remarks and tap him on the arm or shoulder. I remembered that was how I lost jobs in the past. This occasion wasn't going to create the same error. I didn't want history to repeat itself.

Life was always a learning experience. I comprehended the hard facts. For people who are very racist, if they didn't want to associate with others, then let it be. You can't force them. If the person made a racist remark or was physically and/or verbally aggressive, then bring it up to your supervisor.

If he or she said, "Oh, let it go. They're only playing with you." Then after reporting to human resources, if they too decided not to act, you could go to an upper channel, meaning bringing a lawsuit. Most individuals don't understand racist and sexual remarks. Most managers don't take it lightly. It's a very serious matter.

On the other hand, a person had to understand that working in blue-collar, dead-end jobs, which are very low paid, especially in warehouses and receiving docks, racism, bigotry, and sexual remarks very common. You just need to have a little tolerance.

I experienced this in every job. There's always one or two jackasses. You cannot be good friends—buddy buddy—with everybody. Not all individuals possess well manners. Not all are friendly, nice guys. The main objective is to come in, do your own work, and, if able to, then give coworkers a hand.

Some days, I bumped into Bob in the break room. One day, I saw him reading a book, maybe a war novel. I showed him that I purchased a World War II aircraft carrier book. He told me he served in Vietnam.

I asked him, "What rifle did the troops use during the war?"

He said, "The M16."

I said to him, "The problem with the M16 is that it jammed sometimes." This means the gun wouldn't open fire, costing the lives of many servicemen. I told him, "During the second World War, the M1 carbine, the US Army standard, was the best rifle."

He said, "If a person got hit by an M1 rifle bullet, hoping to survive was a very slim margin."

Then both of us brought up a funny comment. During the Korea War, when US forces were shooting invading Chinese armies, they came like human waves. The American 50-caliber machine gun needed to be cooled by water.

I asked him, "What happened when there's no water to cool the gun?"

He said, "The soldier standing in front of the gun urinated on it."

Afterward, we both started laughing.

What made it even funnier, he said, "It's no joke, which is the absolute truth to the story." As we headed back to the stockroom, he said, "Johnny, you are no longer doing backroom stock. You're going to be out on the sale floor, doing zoning. It's easier than backroom stock. Just pick up all the loose items, and use your gun to scan and place it in it proper location."

"Well, I am going to miss you, Bob. You are a good guy."

"Don't worry, Johnny. I'll be around. I'm not going anywhere. I'll be here. You'll see me. Go to Ronald in HR. He'll have your schedule."

I was going to miss those guys and Bob in the back stock. They were a great bunch of guys. Once I explained to Little Sean and Fritz, "The problem with most people is that they are too hyper on the job. They don't know how to relax a little. There's nothing wrong in making money. The most important thing is your health. No matter how much money you have in your account, when a person dies, he can't take the money to his grave."

They agreed with me and started to laugh.

I went on to say, "Life is very short. We don't know how much time we have on the earth. Maybe after work, catching my bus, I can go out and get run over by a car, and that will be the end of me. In life, everybody needs to have a little sense of humor because life is very short indeed."

"You hit it right on the nail, Johnny Quest. Give me five," Little Sean said.

I hated to take the N20 bus. It was always crowded. Every morning, no matter how early I woke up, by the time I got to the station, about more than ten people were waiting in line ahead of me. Even by five thirty in the morning, it was crowded already.

Coming back to Flushing, it was packed, very dense like a sardine can.

Some of the bus drivers were pretty nice. Then some were considered to be nasty, rude, and cruel. They couldn't care less to answer your question, like the folks who worked for the MTA. They carried this attitude that the general public owed them something. Somehow, I was sick and tired of these people's attitude. About two or three times a week, they got into a physical or verbal confrontation with each other due to the limited amount of space in the vehicle.

Most of the individuals who took the vehicle were mainly blacks, Latinos, and Asians. On one occasion, I bumped into a black fellow, whose occupation was a security guard. I got out of Target on a late Saturday afternoon, and to my surprise, while waiting for the N20, three or four buses passed by. Not a single N20 came by. This didn't look good. I was getting nervous with butterflies in my stomach. I felt like I was being stranded out in Long Island, so I approached this person.

He spoke to me nicely, "There's no N20 after a certain time on the weekend. You need to catch one of these buses, which would take you to Clock Tower Roslyn. From there, take the N21. It will leave you off directly at Main Street in Flushing."

Afterward, we struck up an interesting conversation. We agreed why white folks kept moving out of the cities. We said blacks and minorities moved out to the suburbs also.

He said, "Escaping the problem is never the best solution. We must learn to deal with the issues because, no matter where you go, the problem is going to be with the person. There is public transportation that will take minorities and poor folks to the suburbs."

I asked him, "Where do you live?"

He said, "Great Neck."

"You must be very rich. You know how much the houses cost over there."

"No, I am not rich at all. I need to have two jobs in order to make end meets. The more I earn, the more Uncle Sam takes away from my paycheck."

"Well, you know the familiar expression in America. There's no free lunch," I said.

He started to laugh.

I said, "While at Queens College, my professor said that poor folks and minorities are getting government grants to pay for their tuition, but once they graduated, if they found a job, no matter who you are, they couldn't get away. They must pay taxes to Uncle Sam. That's what we mean by no free lunch in America."

We hopped on the bus to Clock Tower and discussed about how the wealthy individuals living in Long Island and the expensive property taxes were paying for the school system and city planning. As the vehicle approached Great Neck, we said farewell to each other.

Well, it was another good day at Target Hicksville.

I was off to my new job the next day, zoning. It wasn't a glamorous job. It was kind of boring, a lousy waste of time. On the other hand, I felt like a tank commander, overseeing the front line of the battlefield. I imagined myself in a war game when taking loose merchandise on the floor. It was like removing land mines on the battlefield.

One day, I didn't had my name tag on.

Mitch, the store manager, wasn't too happy. "Where's your name tag?"

I answered him, "I left it at home."

"Please go to human resources and put one on. It's important for you to have a name tag." I liked Mitch. I thought he was a very cool manager. If a person were slow or didn't pick things up right away, he didn't get on that person's case. If you were new to the department, he had compassion and understanding.

Sometimes when it wasn't too busy, I encountered some interesting conversations with him in the break room.

I said, "You must be a very wealthy man, being the store manager."

"No, not really, Johnny. The cost of living is very high in Nassau County. Property taxes are tremendously high."

"What kind of job did you have before you were employed with Target?"

"I used to have my own business."

"What kind?"

"We manufactured clothing and ties."

"Was it a big market? Did you make a lot of money off it?"

"It was fair. Some periods, we did well. At times, it was similar to many enterprises. It was considered to be slow."

He was one cool executive, even during his break.

One day, I needed to speak to Ron from receiving. He was having a cup of coffee with Jennifer. He felt kind of shocked.

He told me to pull up a chair and asked me, "How could I help you?"

I memorized all the guys in zoning. In the electronics department, I believed Rich was the leader of the pack. Finny, there was a super cool dude. There was Marvin, and Luis, who was nicknamed Luis the Latino Playboy. Anna, who worked for Starbucks, was laughing her head off.

On one occasion, when I was so busy with my work, Luis would say, "Johnny, you didn't say hi or good morning to me."

"I am so sorry, Luis. I just forgot. It won't happen next time."

"You better be, Johnny. There's no excuse. You're in my department."

I knew he was only joking, wanting to be a wise character.

Out of the blue one day, he brought lunch for me. Whenever we were on our break, I wished to repay him by purchasing a soda and potato chips. He would always turn it down. In my heart, I viewed this person as really having the heart of giving without expecting anything in return. He possessed a real true heart. In most business environments, when an employee helped out another, a person expected something from each other, for example, a coworker purchased a cup of coffee or lunch. There was exchange of favorites, but not in the case of Luis. Later on in life, he taught me the true gift of giving from the heart.

One of the major difficulties of zoning was that you could never get your work done. The difficult of being out on the sale floor was that you had to deal with the customer. In every retail service, no matter what, they were your first priorities. It didn't matter how demanding they expressed. We had to tend to their needs.

Because I was still new to the store, I had a feeling of embarrassment. I didn't know where to direct the client. For example, when one customer asked me a question, before I could answer his question, another would drop by to ask me where certain stuff was located at.

There was a cool dude named Sonny, a really big help to me. He answered most of the customer questions when I didn't know where and how to direct them. I was working in Blue World, which consisted of electronics, toys, gardens, power tools, automotive, camping equipment, school supplies, videos, and CDs. Later on, I learned the trick, electronics were arranged in the alphabet E section, toys and games were in G section, school and home supplies were in H or R sector, and videos and CDs were situated in C and D areas.

There was a very pretty intern named Judy. This was the advice she gave to me. She was a very nice person. Sometimes, she handled a few items on a cart load of stuff and pushed it to the floor.

She said, "Johnny, I am not rushing you. Don't worry about making errors. Please, if you aren't sure, just ask one of the employees."

"Wow, what a nice and sweet thing to say, coming from a pretty girl," I said to myself.

There were about two to three occasions when I didn't take my full forty-five minutes. She saw me going into the break room.

She followed me and told me, "Johnny, you forgot to take your full forty-five-minute lunch break."

"I am sorry. Sometimes when it's too busy, I often forget," I said.

"That's perfectly okay. I understand," she said.

That was the final time I saw or spoke to her. She was an intern who stayed with us for about ten weeks. They were college students, employed for the summer so they could pay their tuition. Upon graduation, they were promised an executive position with Target.

It was sad to see Judy leave. She happened to be one of the best LODs, or leader of department. Like they say, "Autumn leaves must fall. September comes, and school is just around the corner for a lot of these young kids." What could I say? She vanished into the divine wind.

Zoning wasn't working out for me. A majority of coworkers knew right away where most of the products belonged to. I was not very productive in this area of work. Somehow I tried my best to place things in their proper order. I don't exactly remember, but I got some wonderful comments from coworkers and managers that I picked things up from the floor. Some days, there were no reshop, meaning putting stuff according to their department sections, so it was very slow.

From those periods on, I looked forward to having the forty-five-minute lunch and ten-minute breaks. I usually bumped into Finny in the break room. Conversations happened to be very interesting. Of course, most discussions centered on women.

I spoke to him, "Some girls in Target have a bad, nasty attitude. Young idiots. Real immature."

He definitely agreed with me. On the other hand, one or a couple of bad apples won't spoil the whole bunch.

We said, "There are some fine women in Target."

One thing I admired Finny's statement is that he didn't think dating female coworkers was considered the wildest thing to do in any working environment.

He said, "Whatever you do within the company, when it comes to business, put it in perspective."

While many kids graduated from high school around the age of seventeen or eighteen, Finny and I didn't graduate until we were twenty. We both struggled with basic English and math. I told him that I used to cheat in school. He gave me a dose of good laughter and mentioned that he could care less. I assumed he probably did the same stuff.

In one situation around 1984, in a retail department store, I used to be called Alexander. I had just completed an employment application.

The interviewer said to me, "Oh, Mr. Wong, you're behind." She was very nosy. "What do your parents do for living?"

"My father worked in a Chinese restaurant, and my mom was employed in the garment district."

"Well, the government gave you the opportunities to go to school."

Nowadays, if any interviewer asked me those questions, I'd said to him or her, "That's not a very nice thing to say, and it's really none of your business what my parents do for a living."

He definitely agreed with me, saying they did the same crap to him.

"Everyone in Target, let's all say three cheers for Finny, three cheers for him indeed," I said.

Unfortunately, he said, "There are those authority figures who abuse and say ridiculous stuff to give individuals low self-esteem. They enjoy abusing their power over people."

His answer was absolutely right from my past working experiences. I saw it all the time. The way I see it, we all want to get ahead in life. There's absolutely nothing wrong in aiming for a promotion and getting more money. On the contrary, let's not do it in a way to step on other employees' shoes or abuse your authorities to make yourself look good in front of upper managers.

Then there are those workers who loved to kiss other people's or managers' asses in order to get ahead and please themselves. These individuals are very selfish. They aren't concerned about helping others, only assisting themselves. They are not working for the interests of others. They are only looking out for their own.

Come September, children, teenagers, and adults returned to school. Older men and women reported back to work. The autumn season was probably one of the saddest calendar periods of the year. The warm, gentle, cool summer breeze no longer communicates to us. Instead, the cruel, angry wind of autumn comes knocking on our doorstep. It carries a message of anxieties because, at this moment in our lives, we are either being successful in school or our career.

Returning back to school was considered one of the most depressing periods of my life. Nobody wanted to look forward to six hours situated in a building, while going back home, there was homework and exams to be studied. In college, one repeats the same boring life of elementary, junior, and high school. The bright spot with university life is that you get to choose your major. You enjoyed your study, but it wasn't an easy case. You had to pick an academic field where there would be employment opportunities.

In college, if you're not black or a minority, there wasn't any financial aid you could qualify for. The only bright spot was if the school provided a scholarship. If not, a person needed to rely heavily on student loans, which was 8 percent interest rate and must be paid back in six months upon graduation. During 1987, I borrowed around $1,500 to attend New York Tech in Old Westbury, Long Island. I never finished the program and dropped out. The next year, I received over a hundred mails, demanding I pay back the loan.

I could see Target was gearing for the fall season. A large section of school supplies was being delivered to the back stockroom. It consisted of books, pens, pencils, notebooks, loose-leaf sheets, magic markers, crayons, rulers, protractors, inks, and maybe some textbooks.

Summer clothing, such as shorts, swimsuits, and short-sleeved shirts, were being pulled off from the shelf and being replaced with long-sleeved shirts, dress pants, dress suits for women, two-piece suits for men, working shoes, and, finally, designer jeans.

Also appearing in the picture were the arrival of new employees. I couldn't remember any of their names, but most were very pleasant. I greeted them by having short conversations. Somehow, we felt we were soldiers of employees getting ready to meet the demands of many clients, yet our nation economy was collapsing due to the overspending on the Iraq War. I didn't know how much capital or money was in the American wallet. I had some beliefs that our beloved nation was losing jobs as years approached. We were building fortresses of meeting the customer satisfaction.

The next day, Ron from human resources asked me to come into his office for a chat. I was very nervous. As soon as he told me what happened, my knees and body started shaking rapidly, hoping he wasn't going to give me the ax (can me). Besides, I might be slower than the average person and making huge mistakes. I always answered the call by working as hard as anybody else. I felt my throat really tighten. My body was very tense. I noticed some employees greeted me. I was so tense. I could hardly breathe and opened my mouth to say hi.

By ten in the morning, I arrived at his office.

He greeted me. "Hi, Johnny. How's everything? Please tell me how you are doing."

I was so shocked by his pleasant statement though. He might be saying, "How come things aren't working out?"

"I've been hearing reports. You haven't been concentrating and not producing well in your work."

Not one of those words was directed at me. Instead, he was interesting in seeing if I needed any accommodation.

"I heard you have a disability. It's quite okay. You have full confidentiality. I won't leak this information to anybody."

"Are you possibly sure about this? Because if you do, I will be out of a job. Could you please guarantee you'll keep it shut to the LODs?"

"Please don't worry, Johnny. You have absolutely nothing to worry about. You have my full guarantee. There's an opening in the freezer and frozen goods department. Would you be interested?"

"All right."

"No problem. How flexible are you? Could you arrive around six forty-five or seven in the morning at the receiving dock?"

"No sweat at all. I just need to wake up a little earlier."

"There's not too much stress or thinking involved. You just need to make sure to put the food in its proper place. Please report to Ron in receiving. He's a very nice person. If you don't pick things up right away or are a bit too slow, he's very understanding. He won't yell, scream, and get on your nerves. I am afraid that will be all. Are there any questions? If not, I wish you the best of luck, Johnny."

"Thank very much."

As I was exiting human resources, lo and behold, guess who I bumped into. None other than Ron himself.

"Hey, Johnny, did you spoke to Ron in HR?"

"Yes, I just did."

"How about working in the freezer and frozen goods department? Most of the guys are okay. If you don't understand or have any questions, please ask. We will be more than happy to help you, Johnny."

Before I headed off to the frozen goods department, I decided to purchase a candy bar. At first, I was frightened to go to a black cashier, so I said, "I have nothing to lose. If she isn't friendly or nice to me, then God, please let me not say any harsh, angry words to her. Let me ignore her and walk away."

"Hi, Johnny. How are you? That's all you buying?" I could tell by her accent that she was Jamaican. "You know, I am going to call you Johnny Carson from now on."

"Well, good luck to you, because Johnny Carson is dead, no longer around," I said.

"In that case, you could be the Chinese Johnny Carson."

Afterward, we started to laugh. Her name was Sophie.

During my stay in Target, she was considered somewhat a mother figure. I was very happy. She considered herself to be a Christian. I really admired her faith in the Bible, her walk with the Lord, and her words of encouragement she poured on me during difficulties in my life. She was usually happy, very spiritually uplifting.

I told her about some of the harsh things I did in life and having a vengeance heart.

"It doesn't matter, Johnny. God still loves you. He died for your sins. I am glad you're honest with him," she said.

"Well, I don't think God would honor a person like me, one who said evil prayers wishing those who hurt me would perish in a car accident."

"Johnny, God knows our heart. We are not perfect. When we fail, we must confess our sins, and he's forgiving us."

There was time that I was so upset with certain individuals back in Kansas City. I couldn't concentrate at my work, and I would say to her, "Sophie, please don't tell me how much God loves me because I am suffering so much."

She had that pleasant smile on her face and said, "Johnny, don't worry, you'll be okay. I pray for you."

Later on, I introduced myself to Terrance. He was a wisecracking, funny dude, a pretty friendly individual.

He told me, "We get delivery on Mondays, Wednesdays, and Fridays. They arrive around seven in the morning." He showed me where the cooler was located right next to the freezer. "The yogurt, milk, and dairy products belong in the cooler, while ice cream and frozen foods stay in the freezer."

He also taught me certain ways to pull the skids. Those skids were loaded with goods, and they were very heavy indeed. Friday was the worst day of them all. We got the most delivery on that day. We got butter, juice, yogurt, ice cream, meats, frozen foods, milks, Jell-O, eggs, and cheese. You name them, everything came on Friday.

We had a great crew in this department: Tim, Chris, John, and Ray. Terrance put me in charge of the yogurt, Jell-O, eggs, juices, and cheeses. Chris was a college dude. This job happened to be his bread and butter. He needed to pay for his tuition. Besides working at Target, his other employment was in the movie theater by the mall. By the time he finished working through the day, he felt like passing out because he put in an average of thirteen hours a day.

He went to Stony Brook University in Long Island, still a pretty decent college. The only difficulty was that he resided on campus. Many nights, he went without sleep because they turned on the loud music, similar to blasting the stereo to full volume.

I often referred to Chris as Superman. He looked in some way like Christopher Reeves. Chris was your typical all-American kid. He symbolized the American work ethic. He was willing to tackle any job and go to school during the fall season. He reminded me of some of the past New York senators while, during the summer, they labored tremendously a number of hours and, come September, headed off to school.

Tim was a great teenager, a high schooler, a cool dude. He and I usually had one or two good jokes in regard to certain groups of women and races of people.

A slimy character told me, "Johnny, do the best you could. Don't take any crap from anybody."

John, a wise guy character, often possessed a funny joke. If he didn't like certain employees, he blasted, criticizing them and giving them a bad rap. Somehow, he and I were a great team. He taught me everything: the ins and outs, the ropes in the department, the dos and don'ts. In the frozen section, I considered him the leader of the pack. He was big, but he had a gigantic heart for people. He never condemned me for not putting certain foods away fast enough. Whenever a client asked me if we carried anything in stock, he would be more than happy to assist him. He took real care of me, making sure nobody busted my chops. He wouldn't let anybody get on Johnny Wong's case.

It was fun stocking the shelf with items. On some occasions, laboring as reverently, I felt a hunger in my stomach, so I once glanced at the frozen cuisine. I thought to myself, *Only if Target had a microwave. Let me pop one up and just gobble it down as quickly as possible.*

Looking at those cuisines reminded me of the cooking show "The Iron Chef." Sometimes, I thought of being a chef at Target, cooking for the LODs, team leaders, and employees. I imagined myself swinging the knives, flipping the pots and pans, cooking the meals, and decorating a cheesecake. I viewed myself going up to the stand, receiving the Iron Chef trophy.

I loved putting away the yogurt. Terrance ordered a lot of them, especially during the summer. People enjoyed eating them. Twice a week, they were on sale. Another item that went on sale was the juice. We carried a variety of orange juice. The frozen vegetables and seafood cuisine was another hot product that people normally purchased. During the summer, the ice cream crowded the receiving dock. Customers liked buying the pizzas if they were on sale.

There was time the delivery people came from a brand-name company. When stocking the bread and ice cream, we had a good conversation between us. Some situations presented humorous jokes, but we normally spoke mainly on sports. Baseball was the name of the game. We usually discussed among ourselves. We were very happy those fellows symbolized the good luck charm. Almost every single one happened to be a gung-ho Mets fan. Boy, that really made my days go by quicker.

Even though I had many bad experiences with blacks, in my own personal opinion, the Chinese were the worst at Target, especially the customers. In one situation, I was brushing my teeth in the bathroom because I just finished eating my dinner. As I was brushing, this Chinese old man noticed it and kept on staring at me. I glanced back at him. He wouldn't turn his eyes away from me. We were at a staring match. I assumed he won the contest because he waited for me to turn my head away from him.

In another scenario, one Chinese woman was looking at the yogurt stack, I asked her, "Can I help you find something?"

She totally ignored me. The other time, moving the garbage cart, I told her to watch her back. She wouldn't move her shopping cart, so I didn't really have enough room to maneuver. The garbage cart hit her shopping cart slightly. One time, I was putting away some frozen foods. The next thing, as I turned around, this woman tried to trash some of the Target frozen meats to the garbage cart.

I said, "Please don't do that. That's not very nice."

She asked me if she could have the shopping cart. She was holding two carbine bins.

I said to her, "We needed to dump the empty carton. You could obtain one near the parking exit."

She wouldn't go away until she had the shopping cart. I finally gave in to her demand. Guess what. I found it hard to believe that she mentioned two simple words of "Thank you" to me. Even to this very day, as I am writing my manuscript, I still find it hard, coming from a Chinese person.

Friday was the worst day for me. Most of the day, I was alone by myself, moving those skids. They were heavy as hell. Some of the employees were nice enough to help me move the skids. They pushed the back while I dragged the heavy load.

One day, Gina noticed I was struggling. Out of all the women in Target, she was the only one who asked me if I were okay. Somehow those words meant more to me than the physical assistance, but now, please don't get me wrong. I was always happy for whomever could help me to move those skids. When she asked that, she was worried and showed some sort of concern for me. Words could be very strong. They hold tremendous impact. If used in negative terms, they will totally destroy a person emotionally. In contrast, Gina's words were showing care and kindness.

I always liked Gina. She just possessed this personality where she was plain downright friendly. She was happy to be around coworkers. I never saw her once having any angry words with any clients, managers, or employees. Maybe once I said hi to her did I not get a response from her. In another situation, she said, "Thank you, Johnny." I didn't respond the first time. She repeated again, and I answered her, "You're welcome."

When I viewed her attributes, there was a message in my mind. "Johnny, you might have had many bad experiences with blacks. I perfectly understand how you feel, but not all blacks are bad, condemned criminals. We're just like normal individuals struggling financially. We're in the same boat as you. We're not perfect people. Sometimes we could be nice. We have our rough times if going through a bad day, similar to anybody else on this planet."

I think I got to know Gina when I was zoning the department. Often clients approached me with a question concerning the location of certain products. Right away, I encountered the goose bump. Right away, she didn't hesitate to answer their questions for me.

When I was pulling items in the back stockroom, nobody ever really thanked me for putting their stuff in the cart. She always thanked me. I tried my best to help others as I was throwing my own garbage. When I saw employees coming in with cartons, I usually asked them if I could offer my assistance in trashing their garbage. Some took advantage of me. Even if they had a little trash in their cart, they still let me throw their trash in the dumpster.

That was not the case with Gina. When I offered to help her, she said, "That's okay. Thank you very much. That's very nice and sweet of you. I only have a little."

When I left Target, I was glad I had a friend like Gina. I am very glad she's the type of person that I knew.

There was a dude named Sam. I don't know much about him, but he seemed like a real happy, jolly fellow, going around, smiling, laughing, and cracking jokes. I liked to be around him. He made the day go by a little quicker. One major fault he possessed was that he was one lazy dude.

"Ha-ha, Johnny, I heard you were in the Chinese Tong," he said. "What's the Tong?"

"Are the Chinese gangster?"

"Oh yeah, that's so stupid of me. How can I have missed that?"

At times, I said to him, "You know the Chinese and Jews are the hardest workers and the best people on the earth."

"Yeah, you're right on that, Johnny. Give me five."

"The Jewish people are the number one fans of Chinese food. You folks give us more than a million bucks a year."

"Of course, Johnny, I can't think of anyone who doesn't like Chinese food. I have it about twice a week, especially when I get paid."

Then one day, the unexpected happened. I was caught off balance. I fell from the safety net. On that particular Friday, I needed assistance to pull the heavy skids. Normally on a Friday, I got an average of about four to five skids. I made a request, and Sam promised me, but he failed to keep his word.

As I was pulling the last skid, he finally showed up and asked if I needed his help.

"No, Sam, that's okay," I responded angrily.

Boy, he erupted like a red-hot volcano. "Johnny, Terrance is going to get pissed off at me. He's going to ask me how Johnny is doing today by himself."

"I am going to give you Luis for the time being," he said.

On this day, the crap really hit the fan. The freezer was already crowded with dairy products and goods. I was trying to get the final skid to the freezer, but to no avail. Our manufacturer put the yogurt, Jell-O, cheese, and meats, at a bad position. As I was wheeling in the frozen goods, all of a sudden, the yogurt started to fall down on the floor.

I told Luis, "I am going to get some napkins and clean up the mess."

Then later on, Sam probably saw Luis standing there all by himself.

"Johnny, how come I saw Luis standing there, doing nothing?"

Boy, was I mad as hell. "What the hell do you mean you saw Luis standing there doing nothing? Do you know that the yogurt spilled on the floor? I had to get some paper napkins to wipe the stuff. Besides, you saw Luis standing there. He doesn't know anything about our department, and I had to explain to him what to do."

"Calm down, Johnny. Just calm down. You don't need to be defensive with me."

"I am not trying to be defensive. You don't understand the facts, and I am just trying to tell you."

A couple of minutes later, he returned, this time with compassionate words. "Johnny, nobody is saying you were lazy and not doing your job. Nobody is criticizing you. From what I observed and other people, you're doing a great job."

"Thank you very much. I am very sorry if I hurt your feelings. Please let me buy you a soda." I wanted to make up for it. "I don't desire bad blood or harsh feelings between us."

"No, that's perfectly okay, Johnny. No problem at all. You're fine."

Afterward, I never had any hard feelings with Sam. I don't think I ever asked him for help. I might have, but I didn't have high expectations for him. Sam, in my opinion, was not an evil, cruel person who would challenge you to a physical confrontation. The way I viewed people forever was that, if he or she performed an angry action, there usually was a soft side in him or her. He did come back to apologize and speak some good words to me. The only difficulty was that he didn't really take his job seriously. The things I saw in him, I saw he was your average person in the crowd. He loved to hang out in the bar, create a few jokes, have a drink, and share your laughter.

I needed to be honest with almost everybody in Target. I felt kind of good when he got canned from the exec. But later, I viewed myself as a total hypocrite. In the past, I said evil and angry words, cursing at others and gossiping behind other people's backs. What right do I have to feel good for Sam? If I label myself a Christian, even having hate and negative words against him was considered to be wrong in the sight of God.

A couple days after I left Target, I decided to pray for Sam. "Please, God, provide him a job. Times are hard. There's a lot of people out of work. He couldn't continue to live out of his savings." As time went by, I also had loving remorse and pity for Sam.

During the 1962 Cuban Missiles crisis, even to this day, I always cherished Kennedy's speech. I don't recall what the exact quote was. "We are all immortal. We live on Planet Earth. Somehow we must learn to cherish and share the resources on this planet, or we'll perish."

I had some great news for everybody in Target. From now, I was going to get a ride early in the morning from none other than my college buddy, the one and only David Fool Man Chug. I desired the whole wide world would know David Dixon. We go back when we were at Newtown High School. He was in my earth science class. The way he answered the teacher's question, it seemed like it was coming from a Nobel Prize person. Each response contained a mathematical solution. I foreshadowed his future, imagining one day he would be a Harvard professor teaching chemistry, physics, biology, and earth science.

Someday, he probably mentioned, "Well, Mr. Wong, why are you always daydreaming about girls? Why can't you concentrate on my lecture just for once? When you don't succeed, you have nobody to blame but yourself."

We hooked up with each other while in Queens Borough Community College. I was so shocked to see him there. A real genius like him, what was he doing in a two-year college? He told me he wanted first to get his associate's degree and then later on go to a four-year university to get his bachelor's degree.

We found each other in the Agape Christian Fellowship. Every Wednesday afternoon from noon to two was club hours with a great bunch of people. It was a super time for sharing, studying the scriptures, reading the Bible together, and praying with one another. The first time we went there, a fellow by the name of Paul introduced himself to David and me.

The scariest moment in the fellowship was the day they showed "The Thief of the Night." It's based on a character named Patty. She'd heard the Gospel on many occasions, and she was relying on her feelings. She refused to make a decision for Christ. One evening, her husband accepted Christ in his heart. That night, she had a dream where the rapture happened. All Christians went up to heaven to meet their Savior, and she was left behind. When she woke up, her dream became a reality. I recalled seeing that film my junior year of high school.

When it came to English composition, I sucked at essay. They never gave a sucker an easy break like me. No doubt about, he was like a relief pitcher who came out of the bullpen to proofread my essay. Similar to a college professor full with all these wonderful details, similes, and metaphors, the way he wrote, correcting was poetic in action. The way he checked the error, it was similar to dropping pipe bombs on the paper.

Today happened to be my first ride to Target Hicksville. It was kind of a special feeling. In the early dawn of the morning, something popped into my head, the Beatles song, "Blackbird singing at the crack of dawn." It was a great feeling seeing the moon some mornings. We spoke about the atmosphere on the moon. It's very cold in the morning, while in the afternoon, it gets extremely hot. That's why astronauts wear spacesuits.

I imagined David Fool Man Chug's car as a rocket. New York City was earthbound; Hicksville, Long Island, was situated on the moon. Stars represented the traffic light. We felt we were marching, gearing for a combat mission.

Because this was our first mission on the road, he had a little bit of a hard time finding where Hicksville was. Yesterday, I went to the mall and handed him a map of Hicksville. I told him Hicksville was either on exit forty-two or forty-nine. We finally got there around six forty in front of Broadway Mall. I tried to get in. I couldn't believe it. It happened to be locked.

"Good, now I am going to be late at work. How am I going to enter Target?" I asked myself.

Then suddenly somewhere out of the blue, I saw a Lone Ranger, a black state trooper. "I believe you work for one of the retail stores at the mall and you were trying to get in. Don't worry. Just hop on over to my car, have a seat, and make yourself comfortable," he said.

"Wow, boy am I glad to see you. You just saved my life."

"Please tell the name of the store you worked for so I could give you a ride."

I thanked the state trooper and headed for Target by myself. I noticed the gates closed, so I tried my best to find an employee. Then I noticed Toni putting away some stuff on the shelf. She spotted me and told me to go to the side door. I think she opened the door to let me in.

Unfortunately, I had to deal with Alice, usually a pain in the rear end. I had to explain to her that my schedule wasn't with the Zoning department but with the freezer.

"What is this, Johnny? How come you don't tell me or notify me? If you're not on the schedule, how do you expect to get paid? Am I being reasonable?" she said angrily.

"Well, this woman must probably have a lot of personal issues, and she's bringing it to work. What a way to start the day off, raising her voice at me," I said to myself.

I spotted Abdul and started a conversation with him. "Why are you wasting your time in Target?"

To my knowledge, he went to Queens College as well. I graduated in June 1985. I recalled he started to attend somewhere around 1998 but never finished. He said he was a computer science major but didn't complete. It's important to finish your college education. Without a college degree, it's impossible to find a decent job nowadays. I gave him a couple of websites to search on the Internet. I let him know the MTA New York City Transit was hiring, along with the Long Island Railroad. He let me know he was trying to get his commercial vehicle license.

For people who are nice like Abdul, I don't mind extending a helping hand to them. My belief was that you could be a murderer, rapist, robber, racist, or con artist. If you admitted what you did was wrong, you could see some repentance, a change of heart, even if happened a hundred or a thousand times. They might be racist toward Chinese. Or maybe they're black individuals. It doesn't matter what skin color, religion, or economic background they are. If that person is trying hard to do well in life, I won't mind extending grace by buying a cup of coffee, lunch, or, hell, even some Chinese food.

I said to Abdul, "None of us are rich in Target. Most of us are just getting by. The only rich person is Mitch, who happens to be store manager."

He and I both agreed. Neither one of us wanted his position because of the crazy hours he put in.

At times during the morning, I would normally joke around with Abdul, calling him "Bruce Lee Number One Son." His best friend Omar would be labeled as "Jackie Chan Number One Son." The major obstacle was that Omar loved Bruce Lee too much. He carried too much pride with himself. If I could read his mind, he always wanted to be called "Bruce Lee Number One Son" instead of "Jackie Chan."

Some days, when I arrived early in the morning, I would say, "Ladies and gentlemen, round number one. Introducing Bruce Lee Number One Son versus Jackie Chan Number One Son, live at Target."

Omar usually commented, "I am going to kick Number One Son Jackie Chan's ass."

Some wise guys would start laughing in the stockroom.

As time drew by, my mind drifted away from Alice. By ten o'clock in the morning, I was headed toward human resources to replace a battery on the gun. Guess who was sitting by one of the desks. None other than Sophie.

She saw me coming in. "Hi, babe. Hey, Johnny, it's good to see you."

I gave her a kiss on the cheek. She was very nice and happy. She wrote me a note and handed it to me. It said, "Johnny, I am very proud of you. I notice you are much happier and you have a good mental attitude. Keep it up. The Lord blesses you. Sophie."

On my way to lunch this afternoon, I met a very sweet woman named Joanne, a real nice lady. Every time I went there, I always ended up with pleasant conversation. It would start off with simple stuff, such as talking about the weather.

My first real encounter with her was one day during my noon break. She brought some cookies and was sipping some soda. I noticed she was reading a book on ballet.

I asked her, "You must be a ballerina."

She replied, "Yes, those days were wonderful times. I teach dancing nowadays."

I asked her, "Have you ever heard of Mikhail Gorbachev?"

"Johnny, every ballerina in the world has heard of his name. To be a ballerina and not know his name must be horrible."

"What do you think about those girls competing in synchronized swimming?"

"Synchronized swimming is a combination of ballet and gymnasium," she said. "They need to be physically strong as a weight lifter, move like a gymnast, and be as graceful as a ballerina."

We discussed a little about Esther Williams and her swimming movies.

She told me, "Once dancers reach middle age, about their forties, they can't really dance anymore, so most become instructors."

For some particular reason, I felt Joanne's pain, trying her best to make ends meet for her only child, her daughter. She had a crumby husband who refused to pay child support.

I told her, "Never give up hope on God. He will provide for you. Don't worry. One day, you will receive child support from him."

Her daughter was trying to apply for financial aid for college. To provide for her family, she also taught tap dancing at her parents' dance studio.

She told me, "My mother never gave me any credit in life. She never acknowledged what I did in life."

I said to her, "I really understand your life. My dad said angry words and would indirectly put me down. Throughout his whole life, he gave me nothing but low self-esteem."

I loved getting pizza from her. Out of the entire cooks in Target, she made the best pizza. Boy, it tasted delicious, and she made the best chocolate cookies. I normally purchased the pepperoni. She usually told me to buy the pizza with chicken on it. That happened to be my favorite one as well.

I told Joanne, "Not only blacks, but Asians and other minorities are suffering. A few poor white folks are desperately putting their heads above water. Somehow, the media and press are controlled mostly by liberal folks. They are usually one-sided, distorting the picture. They aren't giving the whole picture. When economic hardship arrived, it bares no skin color across America as the economy goes back. Especially nowadays when the recession hit, the people most affected are the single mothers with the weight on their shoulders."

Some days, I found it hard to concentrate on my work. My mind kept flowing back to Kansas City to Clarisse. Clarisse was a pretty girl. She looked great when she braided her hair, meaning she put it in a bun. Nowadays, not many girls French braid their hair. Back during the 1960s to 1980s, it was a sexy thing for girl to show her feminine side. It's very sad. Almost hardly any women braid now. They just let it hang loose.

My physical body was in New York, but my mental stage was still occupied in Kansas City. For some things, I couldn't shake off what went on in Kansas City. I still hadn't settled the issues from friends and people who hurt or disappointed me.

My main obstacle in life was not willingly to forget or to let go of the past. Some people, like my friend Richard in Boston, told me to not be too hard on myself.

"Johnny, you can't help how you feel. Most people don't know you have a very severe illness. It's very easy for them to say 'Stop struggling with your feelings and move on with yourself.' They don't understand because they are not in your shoes. Johnny, when you wake up in the morning, you don't choose how you're going to feel today. You need to know how much you could handle in life, your limitability."

Whenever I saw cars, dirt, or crowd or heard loud noises, I wished I could return to Kansas City. I couldn't figure it out, but I believed I saw some sign stating the population of Kansas City was not even close to a million people.

"Hey, Johnny Five, how are you doing?" Alex asked.

"The Italian and Chinese gangster go hand in hand," I said.

"You're damn right about that," he said. "Hey, Johnny, how about you buy me some Chinese food on payday?"

"Not right now. I am a little broke," I said.

"Sure you are. You're a filthy liar, and I know all you Chinese folks have lots of money in the Swiss bank, a six-digit figure."

One thing that separated Alex and me from the rest of the crowd was that we were Queens boys. Being Queens boys, we had something in common. We were tough and mean. We didn't take any crap from any of you Long Island folks. We're street fighters, meaning that, when people weren't watching, if they turned their back on us, we'd jump them from behind.

Another common virtue we shared was food. Somehow, many people liked Chinese and Italian cuisine. Pasta is to Italian as rice to Chinese. My favorite Italian dish was meatballs and spaghetti. I also liked lasagna, cold cuts, and chicken with Avalos sauces. The common joke was to marry a fat Italian woman so you'd be well fed.

One of the customers asked him where certain things were. Guess what his answer was.

"I haven't clocked in yet."

I am just going to identify his ethnicity because I want to protect his name. It turned out that this fellow was a nasty, unpleasant worker, a very selfish individual. He was a black fellow who braided his hairs. I usually saw him in the break room. One day, Alex's friends called me "Johnny Five" for no particular reason and started to laugh really loud. I was pretty angry with this wise character. He didn't even know me, and he started to ridicule me.

Another time, I was putting some of the frozen meats away. He approached me with something. I thought he meant the price but spoke to me in a really nasty way.

"Yo, where does this belong?" he asked.

I said, "Give it to me. I'll put it away."

Afterward, we stared at each other angrily. I had no option but to report him to human resources for ridiculing my name. The manager said he would have a serious talk with him. A couple of days later, he spoke angry words to me. As I was leaving the HR office, I turned around, saw Jennifer, and said hi to her.

The next thing you know, this person was walking right in front of me.

I said, "Excuse me." I didn't want to bump into him.

He asked, "What's your problem?"

Boy, this guy had a nasty attitude. I thought, *How could he afford to hold a job?*

My personal opinion is that, if an individual has a negative attitude, similar to this individual, how do you expect anybody to hire you? Wise guys are the worst people in any employment because they think they know everything. I did know if he were from the city. Why come out to suburban middle-class neighborhoods and give clients or customers a hard time?

The following day, I was headed off to human resources as usual, and Alice gave me a hard time. I asked for a small gun because I was in the market.

"Johnny, we don't have a small gun. You use what we have right now," she answered angrily.

There were times I would have loved to file a complaint against her to HR. Unfortunately, she had friends there. I guessed she treated all the LODs and execs nice, so even if I filed a complaint, it wouldn't go anywhere.

Her view was that, as long as she did her own work and nothing more, then she wouldn't give you a hard time. She gave you a hard time whenever you asked her to do something. I had some strong feelings. She had many issues against men. I don' think I ever saw her having harsh words with any of the women at Target.

As I was heading toward the backroom stock, a very pretty black girl named Kareem asked about me.

"Hey, Johnny, are you all right? I am sorry. I heard you fell on the floor the other day. I thought you went to the hospital. Are you all right? Are you fit to work?"

"Oh, wow. Thank very much. That was very nice of you to think about me," I answered.

"Johnny, this job doesn't pay too much. You do the best you could, but please don't kill yourself. Don't hurt or injure yourself. It's very expensive to go to the hospital."

"Wow, do you know this is the same group of people I didn't admire too much, yet Kareem reached out to me out of her heart?" I said to myself.

God could be very strange person. Always the people you hated the most were the ones either reaching out and making sure you're okay and caring for you. Jesus said in the Bible, "When there's suffering, somehow there's also compassion."

Sometime on a Friday, when it was payday, I would go into the backroom stock and say, "Listen, everybody. Today is Friday. Try to guess what that means. It's none other than payday, and go have some Chinese food."

Most of the black guys and women would be laughing. Kareem would be laughing like crazy.

One black girl said to me, "Johnny, we just had Chinese food yesterday."

"Well, today is payday," I responded.

Kareem would say, "Johnny, I heard you are very rich. Your parents own a Chinese restaurant, and you have a lot of money in your account."

"No, you have it all wrong, Kareem. I am not rich at all. When my parents first arrived in the United States, English was not our first language. My dad worked twelve hours in the Chinese restaurant. My mom worked in the garment district. We didn't have a whole lot to eat. Unlike most middle-class Americans, we didn't own too much material stuff. Besides, if I am rich, I wouldn't be working for Target."

After what I mentioned to her, she started to crack up.

The following day, early dawn around ten minutes to six, I met David Fool Man Chug at Queens Boulevard, waiting for my ride to Target. To my surprise, his car was there, but he wasn't inside. So I looked around and noticed he was purchasing something from the street vendor.

"Hey, Fool Man Chug, good morning."

"Hey, Johnny, I am getting an egg sandwich on a roll," he said. "Would you like to have one?"

"Sure, why not, if you're buying it."

It was mid-October. The wind happened to be raw, no longer gentle, and it was harsh in the midforties. Summer was fading away. Nice, cool weather was nowhere in our sight. The message behind the autumn wind, no matter where the person was, either at school or work, this was the time to see if one could persevere in life. One might be in school at midterm time or be on the job, needing to stand out among others.

The ride to Target happened to be very boring. We did not have too much to discuss.

He told me, "If you want to return to Kansas City, you could. The major difficulty is that you have to learn how to drive. NYC has the best public transportation. There's no other place like here, so as soon as you leave New York, to go anywhere else, you must obtain a driver's license, or else you're trapped in jail. If you go back to Kansas City, stay away from John. Don't go back to the International House of Prayer, because Clarisse will still be hanging out there."

He explained to me that running away was never the issue, that what I had was inside of my heart. I carried an angry issue. No matter where I went, I was going to have that anger. At other places, it isn't what's inside. It's internal, not external.

"You think your John Ho might look good on the external because he has a beautiful wife and children. He's got a nice house up on a hill and owns two cars. He is blessed by the American dream. But don't let it fool you. Like everybody else, he has problems to solve. You might not see it."

He went on to tell me about an individual who left NYC to live in the Bahamas. In the Bahamas was a great resort paradise. Some would label it as heaven on earth.

His next statement took me totally off guard. "You know what happened, Johnny? Next, the man went out for a walk, and he saw a person had committed suicide by hanging himself on a tree. Just to say that location is never the solution. If you ever wanted to return to Kansas City, you must deal with the anger in your heart, which is internal, not external."

As I got to Target, Halloween was in the spirit there. Strange costumes were hanging out in the children's department. A whole stack of candies arrived at the stockroom. Putting out the candies wasn't that bad. We carried peanut butter, Reese's, Hershey's, chocolate, and marshmallow candies.

At this point, I felt a little confident in answering some of the customer questions. I would tell them about the E section, where we had some of our Halloween snacks on sale. They were very happy to hear about that.

Putting out those candies was pretty fun, similar to playing basketball, like tossing them onto the empty shelf. Sometimes, I was doing a sky hook and dumped it onto the shelf. Unfortunately, on some occasions, they fell to the floor.

There were people wearing different, colorful costumes. Omar gave everybody a good laugh by putting on a funny mask. When Toni was storing away the detergents, I pointed to Omar, and she was laughing loudly. Some guys dressed up as Superman, while others were Batman and the Karate Kid. Somehow, wearing funny costumes made us feel like we were little kids, hopping off with our parents and going to trick or treat.

My first trick or treat happened to be in fourth grade. In those early days, kids carried the UNICEF box, a small, empty carton for donations for poor children in underdeveloped nations. Receiving pennies was a pretty big thing in 1972. I even boasted how many pennies I got in my UNICEF box.

Halloween never did change that much. It's still an American kid's tradition. It's not just for little kids. Even teenagers come to people's houses to collect candies and goodies. On every Halloween, no matter what age we are, there's still that little kid inside of our hearts.

On Monday in the human resources office, Phil, the store owner, announced, "We have a new LOD, everybody. I want all of you to meet Jennifer."

She seemed very happy and cheerful and responded back nicely.

We just got the new gun in from our manufacturer. I needed to set in the control because I was in the market department. I asked Phil and handed it to him. He didn't have any clue, and to my surprise, Jennifer took my gun and tried her best to figure out the control.

"Hi, my name is Johnny," I said. "Would you like to be called Jens or Jennifer?"

"Jens is fine." She was very pretty. She had a great figure. She was probably one of the prettiest girls in all of Target.

I knew right away that I had established a wonderful working relationship with her. She carried the entire right characteristics of a lovely girl. If I wanted a girlfriend, she was the type I desired.

She was sweet, kind, caring, helpful, and friendly toward all the employees.

Some coworkers badmouthed Jens, admitting she was too pushy. When she wanted something, she demanded right away or went into the stockroom. Some said she wanted to present herself good in front of the other executives.

"Why was she so nice to me?" I asked one of the employees.

"Because you always help her."

I didn't pay too much attention by what they said. I went by how other people or Jens treated me. Being charmed by her beauty and femininity, I desired to assist her. One occasion, I helped her throw her garbage. She was standing in front of about six garbage cans.

She asked, "Johnny, can you please help me throw the garbage?"

"Sure, no problem."

After I dumped the garbage, she even clapped her hand and said, "Yay, Johnny."

Every time I saw her, we always smiled and shook hands with each other. There were times I thought about her and told some of the guys she was very pretty.

One girl asked me, "Why don't you ask Jens to join us for lunch sometime?"

I was deciding about it, but then later on, I found out that wasn't a good idea. She was an exec, so the line must be drawn in any working environment. Don't mix business with pleasure. I don't believe in dating in any firm while working. What you do, you must do it after work.

When I found out she was Jewish, I even kept my distance more from her. During the eighties when I was in Queens College, I had a Jewish girl who tutored me in English. She was very funny, sweet, friendly, and nice. She loved to giggle and sat very close to me. I guessed she was the perfect girl to ask out, so I did.

She said, "You're Chinese, and I am Jewish. I only go out with Jewish guys."

Wow, I was so shocked by her statement. My entire body was frozen. I couldn't open my mouth. When I told her I had a girl just as friend, she kept asking me if she were Chinese. My friend David Fool Man Chug even said to me, "Well, she's being honest to you." It's nothing wrong to be honest, but you can't say racist comments to the opposite sex if they had an interest or desire to be your friend. That was just totally, absolutely inexcusable. I don't care if they're trying to be honest with anybody. At the same time, I was very glad I knew Jens the same way I knew Gina, and I was happy to assist in any way I could.

The old expression is, "If you treat anybody nice, you usually receive the same thing in return." If you're friendly, kind, compassionate, helpful to others, and friendly and greet people, people would do the same in return. If an individual were cruel, evil, and easily angry and had bad manners, very few workers and managers would like to be around those individuals.

I treated Jens nicely. In return, she did the same. I didn't expect to date her or ask her out. I kept my distance. With a woman, that sometimes was very difficult. There were few who happened to be pretty. They looked good externally but possessed rotten personalities. In any working environment, it was very tempting. My solution is that, if some women were very good looking and had a nice body, it doesn't necessarily mean you had to greet them, be nice, or assist them. Don't expect any favors in return. That is, lower your expectations on beautiful women or else you'll be hurt twenty times more.

Not only women, this holds true for men as well. If you performed something well, don't expect the same favor. Unfortunately, we reside in a very selfish society. In America, there's no such thing as a free lunch. Even in ancient periods, favors were exchanged among each other. On the other hand, we can't always be on the receiving end. In life, if received, we must also learn how to give.

For a change of pace this afternoon, we decided to take the Long Island Railroad. For the first time in my life, I felt like some kind of big shot, similar to those top executives working in the corporate office in Manhattan. Don't be surprised. It was very crowded as well. Most of the blacks transferred at Jamaica Station to take the Brooklyn line, while the other crowd headed down toward Penn Station in Manhattan.

The two good things about the train were that I got home two hours earlier. Plus, I had more leg room. It was much less crowded than the Nassau County N20 bus. I imagined myself in one of those war movies where I kissed my girlfriend good-bye and threw her a banquet of flowers.

I imagined her quoting, "Johnny, write to me every day. Please come home alive, and I love you."

Terrance told me to come in a little before seven in the morning if I didn't knew where everything was. He told me to walk around to familiarize the departments. It was kind of funny. As I was walking and greeting everybody, saying good morning, this time it was different. I decided to say hi to blacks as well. Almost everybody gave me a good response. Just maybe one or two didn't.

I imagined myself in the airport. Every department was an airline. I acted similar to a taxi driver, waving, chanting, and asking people, "How are you doing today?"

One thing I liked about Toni was that I didn't care if she came from the hood. Whenever I greeted her, I asked her how she was doing. She normally gave me a polite response. You could say she was even better than any of the Chinese people in the mall. If she were pushing two tubs or carrying a heavy carton, I normally opened the door for her. She never refused to thank me.

Nowadays, I ask myself, "Where the hell is everybody's courtesies or good manners?" Maybe a lot of it was how you were brought up by your parents or who the people were that you hung out with.

The other day, while I was riding the Long Island Railroad from Jamaica, I was going to Forest Hills, and there sitting behind me was this wise little boy who was no more than seven or eight years old.

He was crying out, "Chi-chow, chi-chow Chinese."

"Who the hell is saying this to me?" I whispered to myself.

I turned around and noticed it happened to be a little boy, but I heard his mother whispering in his ear, "Shh, shh, there's a man sitting in front of us."

I turned around, smiled, and waved at the woman. I think she smiled at me.

I said to the woman, "I give you a lot of credit for disciplining your son. It's okay. He meant no harm. He doesn't know better. He's only a little kid."

If his mother decided to join in with him or didn't correct his words, then most people would be extremely upset. When parents don't correct their children and get bad influences with peer pressure from the group of people they hang out with at an early age, it's most likely they become juvenile delinquents.

Every morning, I saw Tom always working hard. I usually called him Tomas. I speak a little Spanish, so Tomas means Tom in Spanish. Another person I usually run into in the morning was Jason. I often cracked a few jokes with him.

"You're one of the hardest-working LODs. Don't worry when I see those big shots. I am going to tell them to give you a raise."

"Oh, Johnny, thank you very much. You make sure you keep your promise. You're like an engine in Target, nonstop."

"I didn't want to be admitted to the hospital because the bills are very expensive."

"You're right. Thank you. I'll remember that," he said.

When one of the overnight cleaning ladies stole my soda, I believed it was the same person who took my sandwich. Because one of the LODs didn't do anything about it, Jason told me about zero tolerance. When it comes to stealing other employees' stuff, he sternly spoke to that particular woman and gave her a strict warning not to steal from any of the Target employees ever again or else she'd be out of a job. There are three cheers for Jason.

I definitely agree with Jason. Stealing from your coworkers is considered very low, a kind of dishonesty. If somebody willingly told the truth, we must reveal not just words, but we as workers need to back up our action. It wasn't long before a team leader was let go because he violated Target policy by giving his employee discount to his relatives, but I truly suspected this woman was not only stealing my drinks and food but also other coworkers' personal items. Still she was able to hold on to her job.

Andy from electronics gave me a ride home this afternoon. He asked, "Where do you live?"

"Around the Queens Center Mall on Queens Boulevard."

We worked the same hours, so it worked out perfectly. He said he was heading toward that direction as well. I offered to give him a couple of bucks for the gas money or buy him a soda, but he kept on refusing.

As I was riding in his expensive sports car, we struck up an interesting conversation, like striking oil. Conversation turned to a gold mine. He and I had something in common, music.

He asked me, "What type of music do you enjoy?"

I answered, "Music before your time, meaning the sixties, which consisted of the Beatles, Rolling Stones, Bee Gees, and Peter, Paul, and Mary. Then the eighties with Air Supply, Phil Collins, Journey, and Jefferson Starship. Finally the nineties with Richard Max and Bryan Adams."

I didn't admire the rap nowadays they called hip-hop. I told him that most of it was violent and racist. I said that, after Richard Max and Bryan Adams, this music sucked. I think he agreed with me.

I said to him, "Music in the sixties was a message for civil rights, antiwar, and bad things, which I am not crazy about, which happened to be drugs. We think songs and lyrics made a person feel happy, and life was too stressful nowadays with everybody trying to get ahead in life. Music could also be a form of physical or mental health. It takes the mind off wordiness."

He asked me if I had any hobbies. I mentioned writing and cooking.

"What kind of food do you like to cook?"

I answered, "Chinese, Italian, and American cuisine."

He also liked Chinese, like most workers at Target. He mentioned that Chinese food was the hardest to cook.

I disagreed. "French cuisine is the toughest because most of it consists of heavy cream mixed with milk and butter."

Luis from Green World, the one who Sam sent to help me, was a great guy. It happened to be my distant niece's birthday today. I believed she was three or four years old. I asked if his sister who worked in the bakery would bake a cake for my niece.

He answered, "No problem."

I said, "The cake is for four or five people."

I explained to him that I was once employed in the bakery while in a summer camp. Up in Canada, I learned to bake bread. Baking bread wasn't too difficult. The only hard part was the yeast. You needed to use lukewarm water. If the liquid were considered too hot or cold, it would destroy the yeast.

I let him know that baking was a very fun, unique, rewarding occupation, in contrast to laboring at Target. Jobs at Target were very boring. Most of the work was Luis and me putting away stuff on the shelf.

He told me, "When ringing up the merchandise for the customers, they fight for their last dollars, quarters, nickels, dimes, and even pennies."

I persuaded him that, when it came to baking, a form of creativity and talents was involved. The design and decoration signaled certain pride for you. Performing any form of culinary arts was considered a master skill and could be passed down across generations.

Terrance and I waged an all-out ugly war with each other. I was trying to kiss his ass by being nice to him and staying late. Sometime on a Friday night, I cleaned spilled yogurt. The day I vomited and had a high fever early in the morning, I still reported to work. I thought he was going to give me a break.

Then one day, I appeared to work, and he said, "Johnny, I am going to put you on the candies."

"What do you mean? Just say that to me one more time." I was mad as hell, burning sulfur like a hot volcano ready to erupt. "I worked just as hard as anybody else. This is not fair. Other employees from our department take long lunches and fifteen-minute breaks. They even take days off. Just what the hell do you have to say to them?"

He complained I was too slow, not fast enough. To be in market, you had to pull away the frozen goods quickly, or else it gets contaminated, and people could tell it stinks. Then the LOD would get on your case.

"Yeah, when your friends or buddies goof off, you don't discipline them and refuse to take any action. You just worry about covering your own ass, like the other LODs tried to make yourself look good in front of your superior. You don't give a damn about us. You're very selfish."

I was so shocked. There wasn't any retaliation from him. He even said hi to me in the morning, smiled at me, and asked how I was doing. I expected some kind of shouting match with him. I carried a full load of ammunition, which consisted of evil, cruel, and nasty. I was even ready to give him the middle finger and say the F or S word.

I was crying to myself, "Help me, somebody, anybody in Target. Bob, Margaret, Justin, Peter Son, Big Sean, Little Sean, Frank, Chris, Andy, Luis, Ron, Ron from HR, John the Chinaman, and even Alice, who I labeled as Grandmom. Finny, Mitch, and, finally, Jens, if any of you have any cold water, please pour it on me. I am burning like a wild forest fire. Please, you guys need to cool down my burning anger."

I learned the fact of life. In any working environment, it is nothing wrong to assist your supervisor or coworkers. On the other hand, don't expect to get favorable treatment, or some supervisor will not return the same favor.

If the individuals saw me kissing every manager's butt, they'd say, "This guy, Johnny, he just wanted to make himself looked good in front of the LOD."

The rule of the thumb is that you do the best you could with any employer. Be firm. There's nothing wrong in offering your service. The Department of Labor in the United States took a survey. The main question was job satisfaction. Guess what the answer was. Not money. Not so much on promotion. It was assisting other employees and customers.

For example, when our yogurt was on sale, many times, they went out quickly. First, I told them that delivery came on Mondays, Wednesdays, and Fridays. Often I would go to the back freezer to search for a particular yogurt brand-name. I climbed over the skid and gave it to the customer.

At times, they asked me if we had any bran cereals inside the stockroom. If I found any, when I handed it to them, I saw a big smile on their faces. Or I gave them a rain check. Seeing a smile on their face really made my days feel much better.

Another whom I usually had good conversation was Donald. He used to work for Grumman Aerospace Aviation. We discussed during the Second World War that Grumman manufactured the F4F Wildcat, and in the beginning, it was no match for the Japanese Zero fighter. The early days of the war, at the Battle of Midway, the Wildcat defended her by flying in pairs, known as wingman tactic, which Top Gun instructors still use today. Later on in 1943, Grumman created the F6F Hellcat. When it first came out, the Zero no longer ruled the sky.

Donald boasted and took great pride in working for this organization. I didn't blame him one bit. Most of us saw *Top Gun* with Tom Cruise. Grumman made the F-14 Tomcat. The F-14 was equipped with a pilot and copilot during the Iraq War in Operation Desert Storm. It proved its accuracy. It carried short-range, heat-seeking, deadly Sidewinder missiles and radar-equipped Sparrow missiles.

Every time I saw him, we talked about dogfighting, which seemed to hold the most interest. We admired the P-40 Warhawk. Stationed in China, it was referred to as the "Flying Tiger." The key element that Donald pointed out, in tackling the Zero, it always dived on it.

"You couldn't dive in front of it. Then the enemy would be on your tail, so it had to dive at the enemy aircraft at a certain angle."

This was a hit-and-run tacit developed by a man named Claire Chennai.

Both he and I agreed that any dogfighting was a pilot's war. Maneuverability, quickness, speed, and sharp reflexes, if a pilot obtained all those qualities, then you referred to him as the elite. Maybe he was called "Top Gun."

Somehow being in Target, we could all picture ourselves as either fighters, bombers, or transport pilots. Imagine the tube loaded with items to be put on display would be the transport pilot. The bomber pilot could be the salesperson, locating a customer and persuading him or her to create a sale. The fighter pilot would be the last line of service known as the cashier when they rung up the price. If a cashier rang up five clients, then he or she had five kills and was considered an ace.

November was here. That meant Thanksgiving was around the corner. New faces were pouring in the store. They were like soldiers gearing to go into combat. It felt like we were preparing for the big invasion. It meant there was going to be more overtime pretty soon.

Strange as it may seem, when I was at high school and college, I couldn't wait until Thanksgiving was here because, by October, midterm season was over. After Thanksgiving was over, Friday happened to be the big shopping day. At night, we usually had a big Thanksgiving dinner at my church.

After the big feast, we all shared what we needed to be thankful toward God. Some would thank God for this and that. To me as a believer, we should always be thankful not just on this holiday but every day. Jesus said, "It is always blessed to give than to receive."

I do admit that, when I gave, I expected something and a little in return, sometimes even their friendship. On this Thanksgiving, I thanked God for providing me such wonderful and blessed coworkers, managers, and friends for me.

Joanne was talking to me. The other day, her daughter was ill with a fever, and it happened to be her birthday. On my break, I decided to purchase a CD for her daughter as a birthday present. It was a CD with songs from 1967. I pointed out some of the lyrics, such as "Windy," "Daydream Believer," "To Sir with Love," and "Both Sides Now." It was our time.

My first taste of giving without expecting anything in return was when my friend Bobby gave me a laptop computer. Joanne told me she couldn't afford to purchase a computer for her daughter, so I told her I would give her my old one for her daughter. She was so thrilled.

I'll never forget that day when David Fool Man Chug helped me deliver the computer to Joanne. She was so full of joy and happiness. To my surprise, even her daughter showed up at Target.

As I was leaving that day, she said, "Johnny, my daughter is here. She wanted to thank you, and she wanted to write you a thank-you note."

"Joanne, that's quite okay. It's not necessary. As long as she can thank me in her heart, that's the most important thing. Besides, I am already late a couple of minutes in catching my train."

She introduced me to her daughter, and I was very happy. That day, I had an electrifying feeling in my heart for the very first time. I had done something good for an individual and didn't even expect a thank-you note. And she happened to be very pretty.

I do admit that when men do something good or show kindness out of their hearts for a pretty girl, they often expect something in return from them, usually a date or dinner in exchange for sexual pleasure. If the woman feels embarrassed or uncomfortable, that's perfectly understandable. You know they have to protect themselves from aggressive men who try to take advantage of them.

I had the opportunity to meet a really nice LOD, George. In his world, he happened to be a real gentleman in the way he conducted himself. Just because he was an executive, he wasn't arrogant, demanding, boastful, or prideful. In every action, speech, or physical gesture, he was considered to be a gentleman in action. He was gentleman perfection.

We were introduced to each other one November morning.

I joked about him. "All you LODs are very wealthy people, including yourself. You probably have a six-digit money market account."

"No, Johnny, I am just like you and everybody else in Target, making ends meet," he said.

One day, he approached me and asked me something in regard to my department. I told him the procedures and that our delivery comes on Mondays, Wednesdays, and Fridays. I told him that Fridays were our busiest day. Most of the time, on that average, we had about four to five skids. I showed him where our candies and grocery department was. I showed him the freezer and the frozen goods and where the milk, dairy products, meats, eggs, cheese, and yogurt were located.

Afterward, I said, "I am sorry. I haven't really assisted you enough."

"Oh, Johnny, don't worry about it. You've already done a whole lot for me. You told me about the operation of the department, where everything was located, and the time and date of the delivery. That was more than enough. The good thing was what you taught me, and I could do the same for a new employee."

"Wow," I said to myself, "this person, truly a born-again Christian, a believer not only in words but through his good nature, he backs it up in action."

As I was leaving work that day to catch my train, I said, "George, you're a very nice person. I hope to see you again, hopefully in this store."

"Johnny, whatever the good Lord has in store for me, I put my trust and everything under God's hand. Why don't we wait upon the Lord?" he said.

I said good-bye to him. I believed that was the last time we saw or spoke to each other. Those few days plus moments with George happened to be a great feeling. On those days, along came a gentleman.

The following day, I quietly announced to Ron over at HR that next week would be my final days at Target. I explained to him that, during the Christmas season, especially the day after Thanksgiving, it was going to be crazy, like a madhouse.

He mentioned to me that it was totally understandable. "I think you made a wise decision. I am not upset or disappointed in you at all. I am proud and very happy, Johnny. You had made tremendous progress. We are very happy for you. If you ever need a recommendation or if you need to return in the summer to earn some extra money, I am more than happy to assist you."

I woke up around four in the morning and prayed for an hour. I read a little bit of the Bible and had my usual breakfast, a piece of cheesecake and a cup of coffee. I took a shower and wore my Target uniform. I wrote some letters to some employees and managers. I wrapped some gifts for special friends of mine.

In my mind, those words kept echoing in my head. "Johnny, today is your last day at Target. No matter how upset you are with the blacks, if they mistreated you, please don't seek revenge. Just simply let it go. You started out on the right foot, and you want to end on the correct foot because, in the future, if you ever need to return or ask a favor from human resources from one of the managers, you need to end on good terms."

I arrived at Queens Boulevard around five forty-five, my usual time to wait for David Fool Man Chug. Just like old times, he brought me an egg sandwich for breakfast. During our ride, we spoke about my experiences at Target, the good times, the bad, disappointing, angry moments, and the wonderful things that happened to me. He knew me being in Target was great working experience. In his mind, he foreshadowed my working experiences would be the key to unlocking the future for me.

"I am very proud of you, Johnny. I think you did a wonderful job. The way you conducted yourself, give yourself a big pat on the shoulder. What are you going to do next?" he asked.

"I don't really know. Maybe take it easy for a while, relax, and spend time with my family with nieces and nephews."

"You enjoy writing, don't you?"

"Of course. You know writing is the one thing I treasure. I will never give it up. It is embedded in my blood. I consider it my pride and joy."

"How about writing your experiences at Target? I am pretty sure everybody would love to read it."

"I don't need to tell you this. You know my weakness."

"No, I don't. Please tell me."

"My English grammar is terrible. My typing is very awfully slow. Besides, I need somebody to edit my work."

"Don't worry. You have a great imagination. If the publisher thinks your book can sell, they'll provide you with an editor."

Before my final day, I made up with Terrance. He was a great guy. To acknowledge me, he never told Ron I was a very slow worker. He never went to HR to report me. He never stabbed me from behind. My expectations for him were too high. He was like you and me, working hard at a dead-end job, trying to make something better for himself, which I don't blame anybody for that. I didn't tell him I was leaving until the day before my final day at Target. I was very glad he accepted my apology. I got to see him face-to-face, and we talked like real men. Most important, I shook his hand.

One person I didn't want to leave out was Ron in charge of receiving. I hadn't spent too much time with him. On the contrary, every occasion with him was very pleasant. He never once criticized my work performance or action. As a matter of fact, I even taught him some curse words in Chinese. The day I taught him, he was laughing out of his head. He knew I happened to be a hardworking individual. Sometimes, I guessed he saw me sleeping at the break room for more than twenty minutes. He never once approached me and asked, "Johnny, why are you goofing off?" He was extremely flexible with me. When I needed the weekend off, he gave it to me. When I needed one day off to go to the Social Security Administration, he was more than happy to.

During his birthday, I brought a Chicago CD for him. I said a funny thing. "It's okay, Ron. I am not going to ask you how old you are. In my book, I still define you as a young dude."

He said, "I'm forty-three years old."

I said, "I am forty-six. You don't look forty-three. You look more in your early or midthirties."

"Oh, thank you very much, Johnny. I'll remember that."

I might never see Ron again in the future, but I always wanted to shake his hand. I mentioned those two words of thank you for giving me the opportunity to work in the market department, and I thought he would be very happy to hear that.

As usual, on my last day, I greeted everybody. I took a glance at the store. Those few minutes held fond memories. It reminded me when I first came in, applied on the computer, went into human resources, did zoning, worked with Bob in the back stockroom, put away frozen foods in its location, and assisted many clients. In my mind, I felt sad for leaving. They said the Target at Hicksville was considered one of the best stores in New York and people were coming as far as Brooklyn to work here.

As I was strolling each department, such as the electronics, I remembered Luis, Andy, Finny, and Marvin. In Blue World, there was Gina and Alex. In the cashiers, there was Donald and Sophie. In Starbucks it was Anna and Mark. In pizza, there was Joanne. There were some of the very nice women. In the shoe department, there was a very nice Latino girl. Every time I said hi to her, there was always a wonderful smile on her face.

I went to the back stockroom and made sure I got a chance to say good-bye to Kareem. She was a beautiful girl. It felt hard breaking the news to her. I told her, "Today is to be my final day, and since it's going to be a busy day, I can't have a cup of coffee with you. I am going to give you three dollars to buy a cup of coffee."

She refused. I kept on insisting. Because I might be going back to school, she told me to save my money. I was so happy when she finally accepted.

"Make sure that, when you leave, come over and say good-bye to me," I said.

The big truck rolled in. Our delivery came around seven in the morning. John dropped by around ten minutes later. I was very glad to see him. How was I going to break the news to him? I knew we needed all the help we could muster. Christmas was only a month away. It wasn't easy. I hated to leave John all alone. I learned the ropes, the ins, the outs, the dos, and the don'ts, all the thing concerning the market department from him. I decided to break the sad news to him during our lunch session because I didn't want to take a chance that he told everybody.

I was so busy pulling in the skid with John that I had forgotten about Kareem. Around ten in the morning, I was headed toward human resources to get my gun. To my surprise, she saw me.

"Thank you very much, Johnny. You're a kind, very nice person. It's been good. I had a great time in knowing you. Good luck to you in whatever you do. I wish you the best of luck. I'll never forget you." With those compassionate words, she kissed my forehead, and we said good-bye to one another.

My final day working beside John was the greatest experience in Target. As usual, we told crazy jokes. Conversation often centered around women. For him, he admired those Chinese girls. He considered them as gold, diamonds, and the crown jewel, while I admired Caucasian girls.

The first order of the day was usually storing away the frozen stuff, such as ice cream, pizza, frozen chicken, Chinese cuisine, and vegetables. It was great to have some extra help from temporary workers. Things were moving at a great pace.

I did almost run into a small incident with one of the black woman. I needed to use the restroom. She was standing there with her shopping cart. When I said "Excuse me," she didn't want to move. Then one of the Latino girls was extremely nice.

"We need to move our carts so Johnny can go to the restroom," she said.

"Thank you very much," I said.

As I tried to open the door, it was locked. Then the woman said really cruel, evil, nasty words. "See, somebody cursed."

I was mad as hell. There was simply no need for such outrageous comment. Boy, she really triggered my anger. I was thinking of saying, "You better watch what you say. It wasn't very nice at all. There's no need for that."

I decided to swallow my pride and walk away while nobody was watching. I closed my eyes and said a silent prayer. "God, I am very upset. Let me not seek out revenge. Please help me to control my emotion, and, God, just let me forgive that woman because this is my last day. Let me not do anything to jeopardize myself. Let me leave Target on good terms."

I finally gave the news to John. No, he wasn't upset or disappointed in me at all. I took him for lunch. Sharing our final meal, he called it the "The Last Supper." Of course he said the F word and some racist remarks to me, but I could care less. It was his way of saying farewell to me.

By three, I decided to go over to HR to say thank you to Ronald. I wished to shake his hand, but the receptionist said he was in a meeting. I didn't wish to tell her this was my very final day because I didn't want some of the employees to overhear what I said, so I gave the gift for her to put it in Ronald's mailbox.

I also brought some present for other members but didn't wish to hand it to the receptionist. I desired to give those presents secretly. I didn't desire to create a big scene.

"Wow, this is great. How am I going to achieve this quietly?" I said to myself.

All of a sudden, I bumped into Bob. I let him know that today was my last day working in Target. I could tell right away that he felt sad. I figured deep down in his heart that he knew I was a hard, good worker the first time I worked with him. We had great respect for one another.

"Boy, I am going to miss you, Johnny. You've been a great help, a great person. I really hate to see you leave. I wish you the best of luck."

I told him I had a small gift for him and asked him to come outside. We chatted just like old times for those precious minutes. Because both of us were great Mets fan, I offered the 1986 World Champion New York Mets book. I knew he happened to be a big Islanders fan, so I apologized that I couldn't find any book on them.

He said, "That's absolutely fine. I really love the Mets. Thank you very much, Johnny. What's your future?"

"I'm not sure. I'm thinking of going into aviation maintenance to fix aircraft. I tried my best to obtain the FAA and power plant license."

He thought it was a very good trade, an excellent field to go into.

Bob and I held a great chemistry. We functioned very well as a team, and I hated to see it come to an end. I'll always say he was the first team leader to look out for me.

He asked me, "What can I do for you, Johnny?"

I told him, "If I ever needed to come back during the summer, could you speak to Ronald if I could work for you in the back stockroom?"

"You got yourself a deal, Johnny. I'll make sure it happens."

We hugged each other and said good-bye.

I stood outside and chatted for a few minutes with John. He gave me a sound word of advice. "Don't tell people you're slow or have a learning disability. Target has been very gracious and understanding in meeting your needs. Not all companies or even supervisors and upper management would bend their backs to accommodate you. We reside in a very selfish world. You don't like it, and I don't like it either. But the reality is that, unfortunately, every person is for himself or herself, but I know you have good heart. You do try your best to assist others."

We hugged each other and bid farewell with one another as I walked away from him. I waved my hand, and we smiled, the same expression when he first introduced himself to me.

It was a short distance walk to the Long Island Railroad train station. I pictured every step I took to the station telling a story of my work experiences at Target.

"So this is Broadway Mall. It's been great knowing this area. Thank you for people, strangers, and whoever assisted me even in the smallest way as possible. It meant a lot to me."

I purchased my ticket from the station and said to the worker, "You won't see me any longer. Today is my final day at Target."

"It's a shame. You're a friendly, nice, great person. I wish you the best of luck."

"It's Friday. Go enjoy your weekend and have some Chinese food."

"Oh, I always have Chinese food on Friday with my family," he said.

I stood at the platform silently, my mind was blank, and then I heard the announcer say, "Track one and two, three forty-five p.m. train to New York Penn Station, Woodside, Queens, and Forest Hill arriving on time."

The train was coming to pick me up. Once again, I was going home for good.

"All aboard. Please step in everybody," the conductor said.

As the train was traveling away from Hicksville Station, my life at Target was gradually fading away. As it arrived at Jamaica Station, the final chapter of Target came to an end.

I got off at Jamaica Station. As I was standing there waiting at the platform for the Forest Hill train, I said, "God, it's hard to say good-bye to all those lovely, warm, nice people I am leaving behind. They weren't just ordinary folks. We had common values, ideas, and a strong chemistry on how to assist customers. We made Target Hicksville one of the better places for employees to work and customers to shop. We weren't always perfect, but we never stopped trying. We never gave up. Indeed, we weren't Superman. If we didn't satisfy our employees or customers, we corrected ourselves."

As I stood there, I couldn't help myself. There was a little tear in my eyes. They said in the Chinese culture that crying is a form of weakness. As a little boy, I cried a lot. My sisters, brother, and parents scolded me. I assumed in Western American and Asian culture that we don't really show our emotion too much. I couldn't care less what other people said about how they got the nerve to say that men are not supposed to cry. It's only women. On this day, I couldn't hold back those tears. In those months, I learned about myself as a person. I got the taste of what reality was all about.

I left Target quietly because I didn't want any big celebration. I didn't wish to create a scene. I think in my heart that I did the right thing by keeping myself at a low profile.

I endured, persevered, and survived to leave Target on good terms each day. I struggled to keep myself out of trouble. That was my true victory. On this day, I could proudly proclaim, "Farewell to Target Hicksville."